The Legacy of the Sidelong Glance: Elegies

The Legacy of the Sidelong Glance: Elegies

Prose Poems by
Michelle Reale

Aldrich Press

© 2014 Michelle Reale. All rights reserved. This material may not be reproduced in any form, published, reprinted, recorded, performed, broadcast, rewritten or redistributed without explicit permission of Michelle Reale. All such actions are strictly prohibited by law.

ISBN-13:978-0692338315

Kelsay Books
Aldrich Press
www.kelsaybooks.com

In Memory of Angelina E. Serrao Messina
Dedicated to her children

—I could walk in this life, having rooted myself in the simple knowledge that she existed.

"The living owe it to those who no longer can speak to tell their story for them."
—Czesław Miłosz, *The Issa Valley: A Novel*

"One lives in the hope of becoming a memory."
—Antonio Porchi

Contents

Genesis 9
A Sky without Stars Is Still Heaven 10
Headlong 11
Not All Who Sit Still Are Waiting 12
And Thus Begins the Cycle 13
Osso 14
There Are Theories for Everything 15
Sometimes a Dream 16
Circa 1929 17
Let Me Articulate for You 18
The Italian Divorce Lawyer Tells You to Be a
   Good Wife and Just Go Home 19
Museum of Memory 20
He Will Be Coming for You Any Day Now 21
The Poet Is Mortal after All 22
The Legacy of the Sidelong Glance 23
Are You Mine? 24
The Dictator of Little Italy 25
The Bed You Make 26
Unto the Breach 27
Right Off the Tongue 28
Sour Fruit 29
The Depth of Field 30
Lament 31
Summarily Dismissed 32
Mythos 33

About the Author

Genesis

A flip of a switch can send pain in motion, though you might not know exactly what hurts. The mind will absorb everything around it even if it does not want to. Beginnings are difficult to explain, but let me try. My mother is on the phone in the kitchen, the receiver held between her shoulder and ear, the long, curly cord stretched taut. Her cigarette is pressed firmly in the ashtray smoking itself while she squirts more pink Lux dish liquid in the sink already full of suds. She never took care of herself, I hear her say and I know who she is talking about. My father's mother, the woman who is a dash in the dark to me. The woman who , my father tells me, *photos do her no justice*; that I need only look in the mirror to see her true essence. That she left the world in three weeks from diagnosis to death. A dirty legacy of the dreaded illness and what it took from her. A life of near mythic proportion seen through a distorted lens.

A Sky without Stars Is Still Heaven

My mother told me there was no Christmas tree that year which somehow seems a sacrilege. That maybe the twinkling of lights and the ever-green of the pine tree could assuage a bleeding grief, that there are some things that would never die, that could go on forever into one age and then another. *But no*. There are random pieces of information that no one knows that I folded away, four-cornered in my jagged heart. Her voice was soft. She was so tall. Her face was long. Dolorous in its length. A life made for pain. A face made for sorrow. I didn't know then I would make it my own.

Headlong

The legacy of the sidelong glance. The downcast eyes. Here is your life! Now there it goes. Necessity could be found in every corner of your father's home, under her mother's apron, in the embrace of her oldest sister's first child, but after that it just becomes something else to tick off your grocery list. The definition of "blessed" is to be born without the knowledge of how trivial your life might become. A little sister buried into the hard ground, the stoic faces of illiterate parents, the ability, but not the heart to replace the one that was lost, as if a shoe that has been outgrown. Bound by cultural norms, from the ways of the Old Country from the lack of anything else that was not already written in the books before you were born.

Not All Who Sit Still Are Waiting

White asbestos mountains and diesel smoke. You are pushed out into the street where everyone keeps an eye on everyone else and news is shared in the crude dialect. Your brother's guard your virtue while they ravage someone else's, usually American girls who no Italian boy would marry anyway. The hem of your dress drapes over your knees, the worn leather of your shoe pointed, long legs crossed at the ankle. While you sit pretty, your *Zii* intone, *brava, brava*. The boys take notice. You are known for your gentle nature, compliant, with no hopes of your own. None that they could see, anyway. Watch, there it goes, yourself soon obliterated for all time to come. Love is a spell, an incantation. It can catch you when your mind has set outposts somewhere else. It wears a mask that makes you think you are lucky when you are not. In the end, it would never be your decision anyway.

And Thus Begins the Cycle

Sometimes angry birds will fly hard and swift, but still, they know where to land. Steerage did not dampen their courage, only firmed their resolve. While you stayed close to your parents, translated and negotiated for your mother who never left the house, your so-called life was moving headlong into what you would never be able to control. When mother and son arrive, in wet woolens and mouths like grim gashes across the landscape of their faces, the man who will be father to your children takes his mother's rough hand in his, plays the rogue, leads the way. One only needs to spit on the ground and shift the fedora down toward the eyes to be obeyed, feared. Is this why you did not object? The grinding that you might have heard was not the cooling of the ship's engines, but the teeth of someone with a firm resolve. The one with blurry vision would lead the one blind with unabated rage. At the time, no one owed anyone anything. But now we know debt is almost always collected. Paid with a life.

Osso

There are fitful meetings. Fateful comings, fateful goings. Days too short. Nights too long. Promises given as warnings that sound like love, but the back of the brain knows better. Nets are dropped. Cages built. Prisons with rusty, bent keys. The downstream concentrations are accumulating, but all higher concerns are for today, not tomorrow. For the quiet one there can be no deep reserve. The fish is hooked. The will becomes dry as bone.

There Are Theories for Everything

Before "the old country" became fashionable and theories were made and laws written to protect the vulnerable, life was just scrape, scrape, scrape. Your mother had two feet of cement that she dragged on the floor from kitchen stove to bedroom, one baby and then the next. The always flaccid breast proffered to another "wop" baby. *They breed like rabbits.* Relegated to the perimeter of the town was not a choice, it was a regulation. *Colored babies and wop babies deserve one another*. Different faces, but the same fate. Here in this town, by way of Italy, by way of the Carolina's. All *pomidori* and bathtub gin. Your father left a legacy of close set eyes, a true mark of the shifty Italian, your mother a fragile factory of gestation, giving birth to frail life after frail life, all who held deadly cells, wrapped in DNA and coiled like snakes ready to strike. All along the street, the colored men tip their hats. The colored women hold their talk to the Italian women with sincerity. In the meantime, you are defenseless against a force heading in your general direction.

Sometimes a Dream

The inability to negotiate a crucial curve is planted early. Where were you when this happened? A little sister in the ground, heaps of dirt, a rosary and a mother who became a ghost in ragged clothing. You and your sisters are groomed with the watchful eye of so many for a similar life. But when your father succumbs from the familiar ails of every immigrant, back breaking work, derision and the inability to express himself, the curtain comes down. Enter a man who is not your father. Every Italian woman needs a husband and your mother has barely recovered. In your dreams, you stand alone, safe. With the slight possibility of love somewhere along the line.

Circa 1929

What you know of men is slight. Downstream concentrations and it seems everyone is going crazy. The man your mother married talks in a guttural Italian that hurts your ears. There are blue bottles he brings home from the plant, his clothes full of asbestos. You shake them outside on the front porch. The white mountains of asbestos are your playground, have claimed rights in your backyard. Magnesium Calcium Carbonate and blue bottles that gleam when placed in direct sun on the windowsill. Here is the test of time. The breeding ground of everyone's unfortunate legacy.

Let Me Articulate for You

The men were bastards in those days, my mother was fond of saying, as if the times have changed. My father with his willow nature, would bend, blink, a nervous habit rooted long ago, nod his head in agreement, because, really, he knows it is the truth. My mother knows how to rake my father's painful memories with a tool that has a long handle. She goes back, turning hard earth, fresh, then damp until what my father had buried is exposed again, memory wrapped in blood and pus filled bandages. Love torn away by malignant neglect. Is this real life? *Bastards* my mother repeats and because of this my father has been the good son, the good husband, the good father, the good grandfather, the Holy Joe, the keeper of memories, with the faraway look in his eyes. *And always afraid of death.*

The Italian Divorce Lawyer Tells You to Be a Good Wife and Just Go Home

Pulled taut and exhausted, you reject the garnish. Throw the plate into the porcelain sink, extinguish the blue flame from the white, enamel stove. The *mopina* that is forever draped over your right shoulder gets hung on the hook. Everything is hanging. The crease between your eyes is deep, deep. A furrow does not do it justice. The courage it must have taken. The shame of a thwarted effort. Culture and community are powerful gatekeepers. The reflection in the mirror looks like you, but something is off. You are all alabaster and molten ash. Like any good woman, trying not to let the cracks show.

Museum of Memory

What happened to all of her things? How easily a life is put into the ground and then every last trace is rendered obsolete. The dead do not need their dresses, hairpins, shoes, but really, where did they go? The lace hem? The milk soaked nightdress? A cardigan sweater, perhaps, a pair of pointed shoes, with a little heel? The dispersal of ephemera creates a persistent ache. I would fetishize whatever she owned. Make my own museum, create classifications and assign each a number, as my professional training dictates. Worship whatever is left of her earthly self as artifacts from bygone days. Straight, no chaser: her husband throws her jewelry in the casket so no one else can have any mementos. Her children's hands twist empty with grief. She is the dead jewel queen, forever resplendent beyond all earthly time.

He Will Be Coming for You Any Day Now

In the 'old country', father's leave, young boys become men; attempt to protect the land and their mothers. Mussolini taxes unmarried men, two shots are fired and the tickets are bought. Shrewdly they will make it to America where their father and husband wait. Extortion was the story that he liked to tell. Anger is wound tight like a deadly spring within a proud chest. She exists. He needs her, but he does not yet know who she is. Only that he will hunt her down until he has her. She is in her neighborhood, with her parents, her sister's, the monotony of every day lays like asbestos dust on her pale skin, but it is peace by any other name. She feels her future take shape without her consent. His charm is the stuff of legend. He makes marks on the wall; counts how many years the vendetta will last.

The Poet Is Mortal after All

The poet's imagination should never fail, but I have my moments. How am I to think of you, and your mother on the ship what you ate, talked about, what you planned? Did you smoke cigarettes? Did she mistrust everyone? You had her sinister brow, the penetrating eyes. I imagine you both withered others with a look, warned them away with a glance. And you. Yes you. You looked back from a distance of safety, so many years later and told your past in bits and pieces like a puzzle to be solved, to a daughter-in-law you liked to twist the knife into. She probed and you pushed back, but you talked anyway. You told her you never wanted to leave. It explained so much. The damage was done. But no one forgave you anyway.

The Legacy of the Sidelong Glance

I do not have her eyebrows. I have made careful note of that long ago. I have my father's, a legacy of his father. My son has my eyebrows, which, are to say, my grandfather's. Which sometimes makes us look mean without cause. She had arched, delicate, small eyebrows. I have the rest of her face, but without the eyebrows. A clash of genes. I feel cheated. I have my father's smile. We both look tentative. *Fearful*. We share all the same vulnerabilities. *You are a stranger, I know, but some things must be said and I want to tell them to you.* Yes, *you*. I wanted a family legacy of assuredness that would show in my face. It has skipped generations. Her smile is my father's smile, which is to say, it is my smile. We are moving backwards now. It stares at me from ornate silver frames. *It is like a shrine over here, my God someone help me*. But she is always looking off to the side. Like life was elsewhere and only she was the only one who knew it.

Are You Mine?

Anything I can conjure about you seems like nothing but mere reduction and yes, because I so desperately wished you left more than a trace, I will speak you into existence. I will maybe invent you. I say, she was gentle. She was careworn. She catered to a man who did not love her. Who ate alone at the dinner table away from his children. She gave him five. That a young woman knocked on her door one day, announcing I am your husband's daughter. You smoothed your hair, shut the door in her face, you, you gentle woman. The alchemy within you was not turning to gold, but what it was is what you are remembered for. Your middle name began with an "E," but not a living soul knows what it was.

The Dictator of Little Italy

Photos were positioned to his advantage. Your feet flat on the ground while he grandstanded on a step, reminiscent of Mussolini. Standing on higher ground was articulation, a metaphor for nothing that was true or that mattered. This is how myths are made, we can see this only in retrospect, but we see it, nonetheless Here is study in contrasts: his suit, wide legs, double-breasted, this wool tie. His eyes taunted the camera. You? You look shy in your housedress, windblown hair, and your youngest child on your hip. Eyes squinting toward the sun? A grimace of pain? This photo will be a testament to a life lived between the shards of glass. Of note: pens in his front pocket. As if he were writing it all down for posterity. A legacy for the children with nothing to say .

The Bed You Make

Your sister never leaves the kitchen. She had the bluest eyes. You all suffered in your own way at the hands of your father, your husbands. Your mother had her own hands full, deprived of a voice, of a life. Your mother-in-law, knew full well your fight, but was grateful, *grazie di Dio,* that it was not hers. Every day you smooth your hands over the chenille bedspread, wait for something that never comes. He calls your name and you run. Your mother put her hands over her ears. *Get on with it.* Sympathy was a luxury, best used sparingly, if at all.

Unto the Breach

Marriage takes him away first. Your true ally. But before even that, you lost him twice: once to the army and again to your sister's house the one who offers him shelter so that your husband will not kill him. As if it was not his own flesh and blood. Let him go to "Lasciarlo andare," your husband tells him with jealousy. And he goes. But we have no account of what you might have been feeling. What you might have said. The fight you might have put up. Tears of arsenic. Even weakness was reviled in a woman. *Expected*, but reviled all the same. You learned surrender to save yourself. The first telegram arrives, signed just like his frequent Hallmark cards used to be: *Forever, your loving son*. You hang your heart by the hook near the door. The blood congeals on the floor below, sticky beneath your sensible shoe.

Right Off the Tongue

In the census records you are "Annie." My father said your name was "Anna." Once, your husband told me your name was "Angelina." I asked him to say it again, and he did. *Angelina.* He said it with a smile. My father did not even know her real name. Blink. Blink. Blink. I said it out loud. *I say it still.* Everyone has stopped listening. Keep it moving. The last essence of her. I will say it forever. Her middle name began with an "E," but, for the life of me, I cannot believe not a single living soul knows what it was. *Breathe her memory into existence, like a plague of locusts that will cover every surface.*

Sour Fruit

An accumulation of derision can poison. Subjugation rarely looks like what it really is. One cannot put too fine a point on this. We are made of stardust, yes, carbon yes, but asbestos dust, too. You drew in the breath of too many heavy sighs, which took the place of any declarative sentence you might have spoken. I was once married to a man who said that a sigh was evil, an omen of bad intent. What kind of bird can fly after it is kicked? Who knew when it took root? Who could say the moment the cells began to thicken and divide, set up a post in your blood. A lump the size of a small persimmon. A blind man could see it coming. Help your first grandchild to blow out the birthday candles and start giving away your valuables. A year in life. You were said to claim nothing more than the fatigue of the world-weary. The woman's lament. The last enigmatic smile of deliverance, but still, the eyes looking in another direction, away from everyone else. Two years from onset was a lie and everyone knew it.

The Depth of Field

Even though we did not exist at the same time, I wanted you to be my mine. I remember one day in a dinette with my mother and brother. I was very young, but already, my face was your face. The waitress was a sour woman, who gave us gum from her apron pocket. As she poured my mother's coffee, a man stood up from his table and looked my mother right in the eye. Through the years I remember his intent. *Are these children yours?* he said. The waitress stopped, cold, still. *They are,* my mother said, her small chin thrust upward in defiance. He pointed right at me and said, *She looks nothing like you,* with real amazement. Over his shoulder, he said to my amused mother *You could deny her! Imagine that,* the waitress said. And in that moment, I thought of you, my grandmother. You would have claimed me. You would have made me yours. After that, for a long time, I felt homeless. Motherless. It became an ideology, but really, *I wore it like a badge*.

Lament

The dying are robbed of the dignity of averted eyes. Everyone owns them. *And yet*. Laying in her hospital bed, not speaking but eyes wide. Her brothers-in-law, brothers keeping vigil. The men as old Roman guards, the stoic gatekeepers. There are no private moments, no spoken words, no allowance for the children wracked with confusion and grief. The youngest only 13 .And then the others. As if it could never occur to anyone that she would not have anything to say to the children she would soon leave, want to hold them close yet away from the breast that once fed them, now fetid with disease. So many pills on the metal bedside table. Treatment or placebo? No one had any hope for a cure. Was life less tender then? Were the beaten down, paradoxically, more resilient? Her sons wanted to lay their heads on her pillow. Her daughter wanted to speak soft words into her ear. Instead, they stood together, apart, forever fending for themselves. Their father, her husband, laments his own illness. It was suddenly raised like the dead, a ghost that only he can see. It took up too much space in the room. Made the meager living she had left like a dress rehearsal for the real thing.

Summarily Dismissed

If death is a release, then what is life? Let's reduce the complex to the simple so we might all understand. There you were. Now you're not. Your children were scattered like seeds. Your husband packed a suitcase to a land of secrets and sin. Well, then, what do we have left? (Dramatic pause). (Possible drum roll). *Exactly.*

Mythos

The abhorrence of the vacuum is an old story, but I take heed. For details that I know nothing about, I *can* and *will* invent. Don't judge me. I can make the world of difference to the tale of this life, by populating it with colorful characteristics that will supersede the old black and white photos. The trace of smile like a grim and bloody gash across her face. I will address her directly, thus: *You are elegant with great wit. Clever, calculated. No hothouse flower. Maybe free-spirited in your tendencies? A little of this. A little of that. Respectful of the world of your mother, but refusing to see limits. The marriage works to your advantage, not the other way around. You do not die of the insidious and cruel malignancy of the breast, but instead, you will outlive every single one of us, usher us into the beyond and then come back again to do something for yourself. You are resplendent in soft colors that soothe the soul. Your jewelry is simple. Your eyes are clear. You are never, ever, ever afraid.*

About the Author

Michelle Reale is an Assistant Professor at Arcadia University in the suburbs of Philadelphia. She is the author of four collections of prose poems and fiction. Her work has been anthologized and her poetry has been published in over 100 publications online and in print and has been twice nominated for a Pushcart Prize. She has recently won the Twin Antlers Prize for poetry, along with poets Meg Tuite and Heather Fowler. The winning manuscript, "Bare Bulbs Swinging" will be published by Artistically Declined Press in the 2014. In addition, she conducts ethnography among African refugees in Sicily and blogs about her experience at www.sempresicilia.wordpress.com

www.ingramcontent.com/pod-product-compliance
Lightning Source LLC
LaVergne TN
LVHW021627080426
835510LV00019B/2785